in the LAND of DANDELION TIME

e.p. rose

First Edition

Studio on 41 Press
Galisteo, New Mexico
www.galisteoliz.com

photos and ink drawings by Elizabeth Rose
book and cover design by Donna Brownell

ISBN: 979-8-9869486-1-4

This book is intended to provide accurate information with regard to the subject matter covered. However, the author and publisher accept no responsibility for inaccuracies or omissions.

Copyright© 2025 Elizabeth Rose

All rights reserved.

No part of this publication may be reproduced, stored in a retrieval system or transmitted in any form or by any means, electronic, mechanical, photo- copying, recording, or otherwise without the prior written permission of the copyright holder, except brief quotations used in a review.

to those still governed by dandelion time
where days revolve gently with the sun

PREFACE

Even now, fifty years later, the word Spain conjures the open faces of my Ruesgan friends working fields of sunlit grain, the sweet grass smell of cow patties spattered in the lane, the gentle clonk of cow bells, and wooden carts creaking past the Bar Juanon, where my family lodged. Eleven summers. Embedded. A time when cows wore shoes and men and women had no use for banknotes, machines or cars. How could I forget?

Those memories… the soughing hiss of threshing sledges gliding a sea of golden grain, gathering the harvest beside our Spanish friends, and of the gentle life they lived before Franco's death put an end to the traditional agricultural methods.

Despite Spain's bumpy road into the twentieth century with its influx of money and machines, the village survives. Though gone the cows, the hand-worked tools and wooden carts, apart from black-top covering the dirt lane, and neat new cottages and flower gardens where barns and haylofts used to stand, all is as before. No additional buildings, no shop, no neon signs, a winding stream, a church, three bars, nothing more.

And when I climb the single track behind the village to the dam, gaze down at *La Era,* the communal threshing floor, I hear no echo of its past, see no faint outline of a corona imprinted in its grass. Instead, goalposts, a knot of children playing football where once golden *montons* of winnowed grain clustered. Cradled below Ruesga's abandoned fields beneath the same red rooves the village looks as idyllic as it always had. And I realize, though things can never be as before, despite the changes, the calm I'd yearned for more than fifty years ago sweeps over me bringing a spring to my step.

Sipping a small glass of *clarete* back at the Juanon, I stare at the yoke, the hand-carved rake and fork, the framed photographs decorating the walls. The black and white image I remember snapping with my Kodak Brownie Box catches my eye. Juan. Our landlord driving a threshing sledge. His pair of cows, half buried, ploughing through the sea of wheat. Staring into the lens, Juan is smiling.

Now that I have lived in New Mexico for almost forty years, I've become aware of the cultural similarities between old and new Spain…. The tools and agricultural knowledge the first settlers of the state must have brought with them to tame this high desert land.

Watching a documentary on the Santa Fe trail I had the confirmation I needed… There in the background as yoked oxen tramped past the camera, I spotted the posts of a cow shoeing contraption… an exact replica of those I'd seen in use in the small Spanish mountain village where I'd spent those eleven summers.

So, cows wore shoes here in rural America just as they had in Spain. I had my proof.

One summer open day at Las Golondrinas, wandering the grounds and small museum, among the display of hand whittled hay forks, yokes, a scythe, single shear plough carved by someone long forgotten, a wooden cart and other tools. I stopped. There, face to the wall leaned a threshing sledge…wooden platform its underside studded with rows of razor-sharp flints. A little smaller than the Spanish sledges I'd spent many a morning cruising around and around the family corona pulled by a pair of yoked cows over the knee-high wheat till the grain fell separated and the stems were chopped to straw.

Perhaps the Hispanic older generation, their grandparents have memory. A family album? A faded photograph? Of how life was before the influx of machines and money. Heard their ancestors' tales of hand-carved tools and working oxen? How they farmed the land? The hardship and beauty of those long-gone days. The peace. The calm. When here in New Mexico as in Spain, people were smiling.

"Tell me, *Abuela,* before you forget. Tell me your story. The one beginning *Once upon a time. A long, long time ago when I was just a child…*"

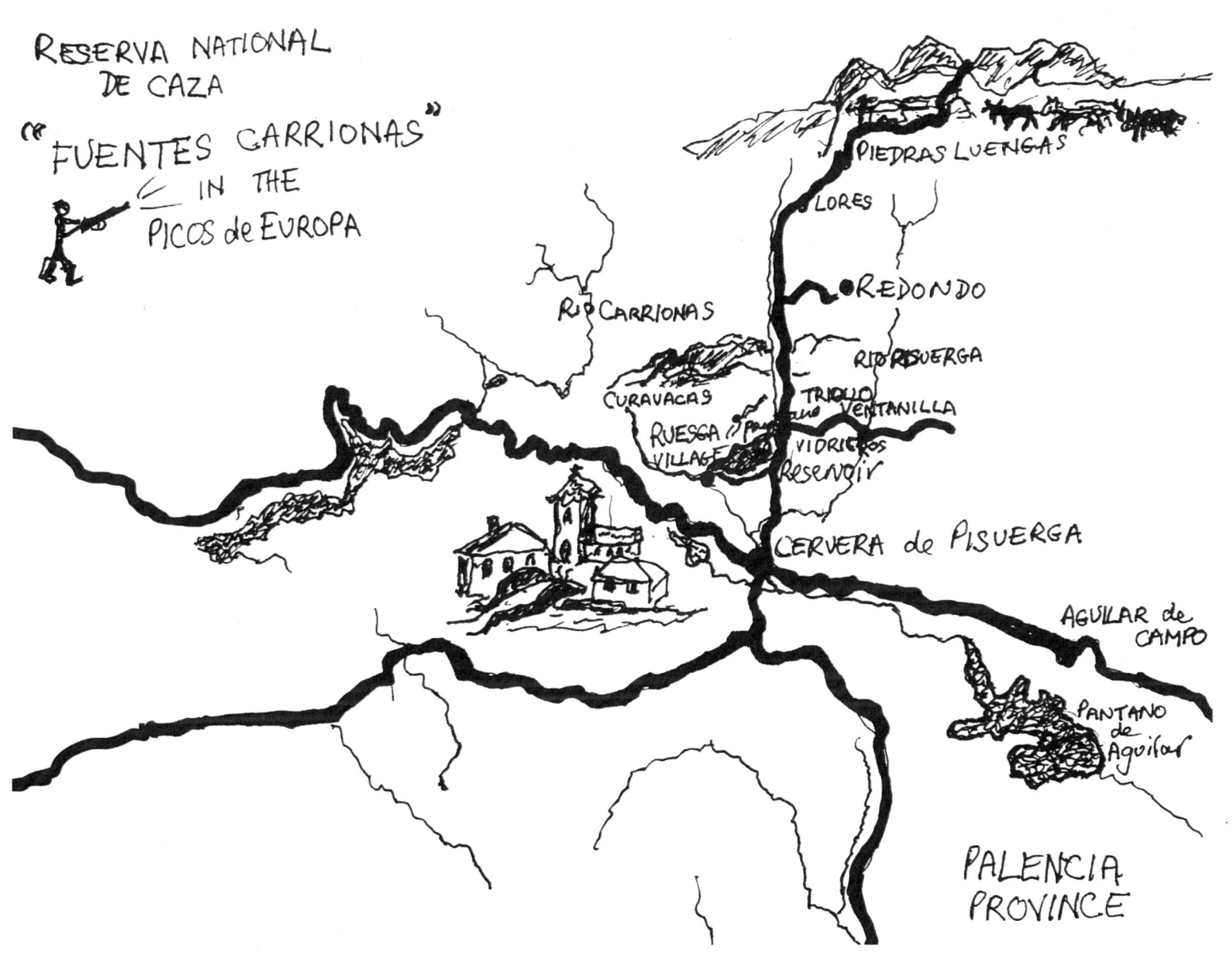

INTRODUCTION

It's just luck this record of rural life in Northern Spain came about. Not from any grandiose plan.

One summer in the late sixties, while raking in the fields beside my Spanish friends, the idea to record a year's agricultural cycle came to me. The time a family needed to produce enough flour, grain, straw, *jamon*, cheese, vegetables etc. etc. for themselves and their livestock to be totally self-sufficient. From seed to a loaf of bread, my thought. All four seasons that it took.

Sadly, the actual ploughing happened late fall after we returned to London, so I only have photographs of ploughs, not the ploughing... Arrow Romano, our friend called the three handcrafted implements he showed me in his barn. My grandfather made that one, my father and me these two, he related shrugging his shoulders as I marveled at their perfect curves and simple iron shears that didn't even turn the sod. Those ploughs were works of art. As were the tools they used.... The wooden forks and rakes whittled from saplings cut from the hedges; the yokes, sledges, carts, shaped by an adze from trees...oak, chestnut and beech; the coops, the bentwood collars worn by calves... everything handmade. Bee hives, troughs, and storage barrels...all beautiful to my eye... sieves, willow baskets woven in the dark winter months, and goats and sheep sacks to hold the year's precious grain. I could go on and on. Owning their own houses, working when they chose...a dream life it seemed to us but of course a totally romantic view ignoring the harsh no-work-no-food reality caused by inclement weather, drought, sickness and times of desperate want.

Every family owned perhaps six or more cows for milk and cheese; a couple of goats to provide cheese, blood sausage and meat; and chickens and often rabbits to supplement their diet. Sausages, cheese were preserved in vats of oil. Families slaughtered at least two pigs a year to make *jamon*, chorizo. The only cash I saw came from selling any bullocks and male calves...and what pesetas they did have, they spent on wine, brandy and cigars and on special occasions, cake. Oh yes, our friends knew how to live. At two pesetas a glass of *clarete*, the men drank small glasses of a local rosé, in the bar. Breakfast, lunch time, the afternoon's *merienda* break, before evening's *cena* and quite often for a brandy nightcap. Sundays and fiestas, white and red wine, accompanied by *tapas*, they drank a whole lot more. Happy but never drunk, it seemed to me the villagers lacked for nothing. You live the millionaires dream, we'd tease.

I carried my Kodak Brownie Box in its brown canvas case with me most days and tried to capture each activity and tool in use. Looking back, I'm glad I did.

This being the late sixties and early seventies, Franco still reigned. Still kept tight control preventing progress. No machines, modernization in sight, our Spanish friends in the Picos de Europa farmed the land the way they had for three thousand years. In a neighboring village I once saw a man winnowing by flailing his wheat with a whip to separate the grain.

Almost from the day Franco died, the old ways died. The influx of machines, electricity, telephones, running water, cars and subsidies to give up their crops and grow potatoes catapulted the village and villagers uncomfortably into the twentieth century. *Mis campos estan muertos,* our friend shook his head pointing to his weed-buried fields. Peace died with them. We no longer returned.

I lie. After a fifty-year absence, we did go back. Just for the day. To my surprise though the cows and fields were gone, the village remained unchanged. Converted barns to B and B's, yes. Electricity and mod cons, of course, but not one new house, shop, or disco disturbed its perfection. Many of my friends were no more but my grown children's friends now ran the bar, boasted a gourmet restaurant on which a photograph of the threshing field hung on the wall.

Sit Sit, they cried in welcome. Clinging to one another so hard we could barely breathe, we wept with joy.

That I knew and photographed the village when I did remain a gift. I am glad for all the Spanish friends we made. I am grateful for their letting me into a little of their gentle lives. To have known Spain when dandelion clocks not watches ruled time, I am forever humbled.

behind
dawn's veil
a village
where man and
beast leave no shadow

slope of red rooves
a tumbling stream
a bridge to cross the watery divide
step into the unknown

no pilgrim but I alone walk the sunlit lane

discover a road with nowhere to go

I watch them
joyous
lovers
on
their woodpile
clacking beaks
flapping wings
a
pair of storks
dancing
celebrate
spring

no living being in sight
a village sleeps

a fallen leaf
a watering herd
widening circles
dappled shallows

caught in the bobbing surf
the tidal wave sweeps by
leaves me spinning
in its wake

up the lane down again
she strolls
where are you going
I call
from nowhere to nowhere
she cackles

marshaling the village herd to pasture
the lead cow plods ahead

the procession silent
the clang-clunk of cowbells
the only sound

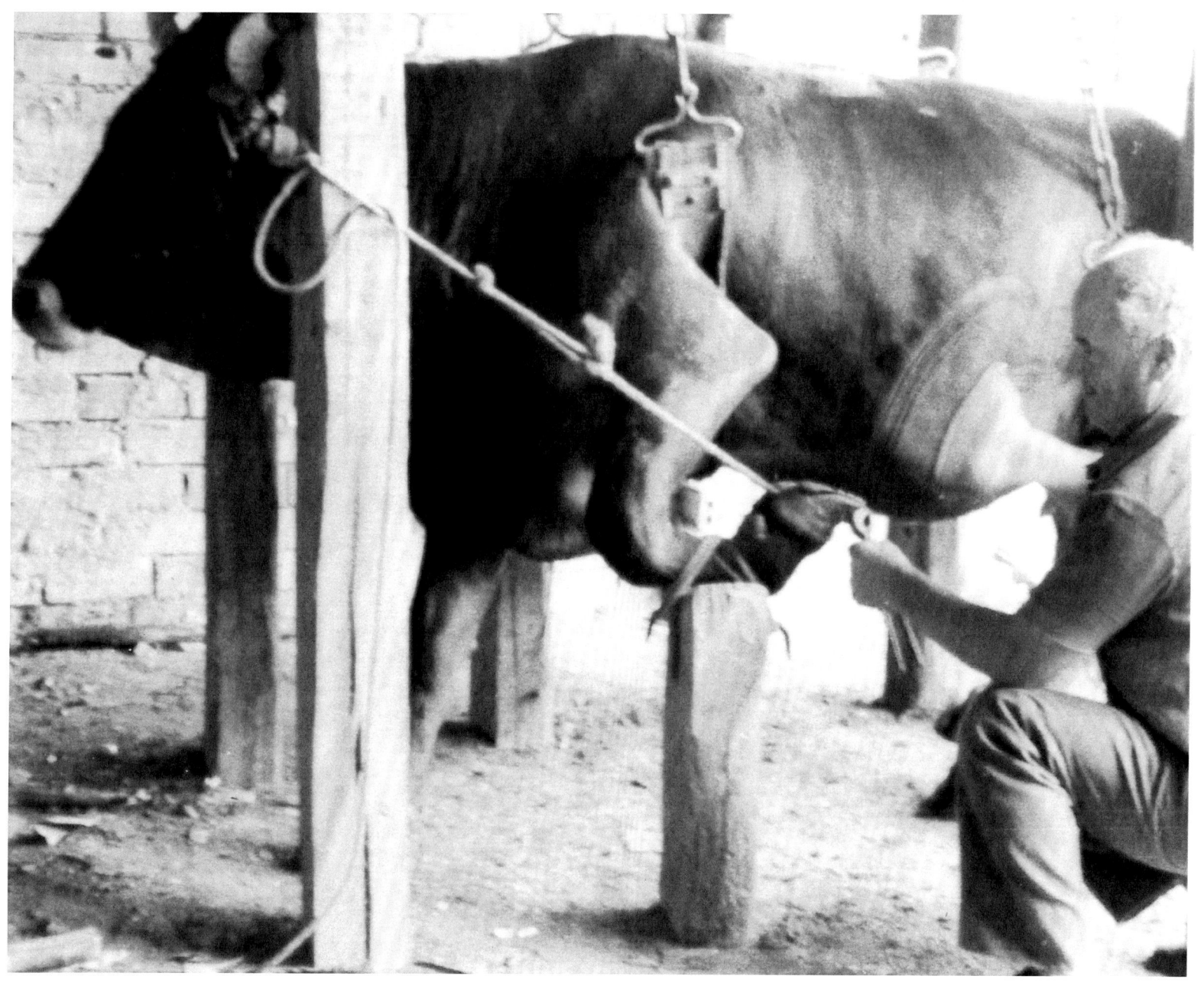

in a corner of the village threshing field
I chance upon a curious scene

a milking cow being shod with iron shoes

tar pools her eyes
slave to her unwavering gaze
he kneels before her

places a daisy behind each ear
does she know
the devotion I carry in my heart

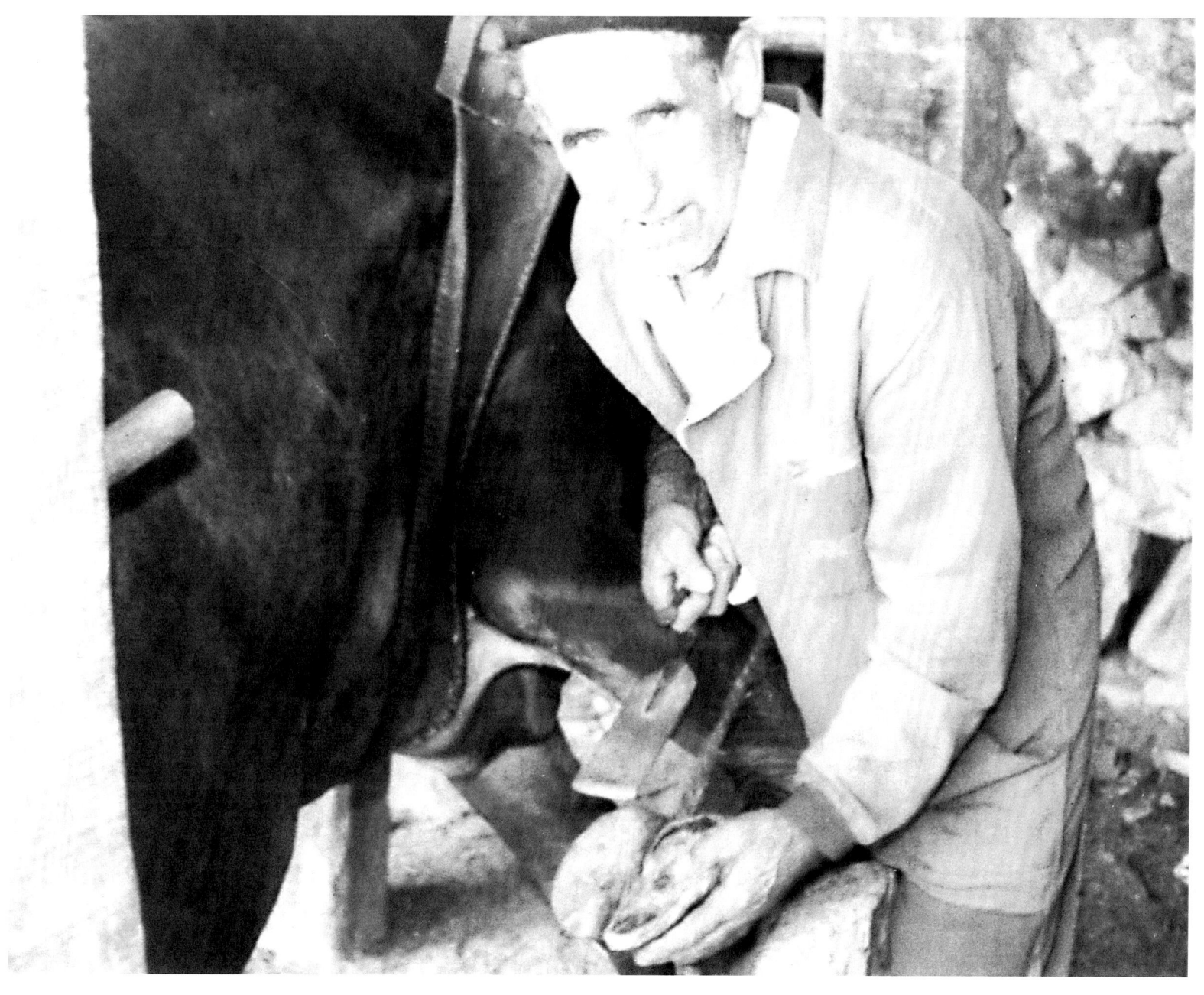

*a cart
a plough to
pull*

*and milk
to
give*

*but for her
my fields would
die*

three generations
three ploughs

unchanged
since roman times

hands resting
on the single sheer

treading
the furrowed earth

he sees his father's and
his father's father's face

the village his world
the place of his first breath
the place where he would breathe his last

a hollow log
a swarm of bees
honeycomb for the taking

kukurukoo
I plead eggs from my hens
kukurukoo
they cluck right back

beyond
the studded
barnyard door
on an upturned pail

I find
the old lady
conversing with
her feathered friend

angels talk to us
in many tongues
she smiles

plump
feathered
alive

the vendor's megaphone
summons

plucked
gutted
pay five pesos more

carrying the
sun in her eyes

washboard
in hand

off to
the river
she goes
to gossip
with her friends

a wine jet-stream
aimed at his moustache
open-mouthed

the show-off slakes his thirst
now your turn
he challenges

thirsty from the mountain climb
beneath the orange berried rowan
picnic erupts to a party

every thought spoken
every secret shared
no need for chatter
laughter says it all

mother blackbird in her widow's weeds
weaving histories in the dark
hibernates until snowdrop's dusting

bottomless his world
catching his
eye
I
plunge
beyond
the reach
of
letters

a chestnut
tree rooted to
the home he loves
the doorway darkens
he ushers us to join him
come on in   come in

happy

if
I have
one word
to describe
these people

yes

happy

is the word
I choose

tomorrow full moon
tomorrow i sow
earth
fecund
fertile
hungers for grain

lone man
a sack of grain
each handful
confetti
over the earth

hammer in hand
tooth by tooth
serrations
zig-zag
the cold
steel
scythe

twist and turn
step swing step
in perfect arcs
wheat fans before
the reaper's blade

gleaners gleaning treasure lost
reveal earth's face between the stubble

hunk of broken bread
wine-filled leather bôta
an afternoon merienda

boys at heart
throw catch throw
grown men
turn work to fun

*now you see me
now you don't*

half-buried
a face

in the land of dandelion time
yellow butterflies sing

herding goats
chopping wood

collecting ant-pearls
from beneath an up-turned stone

in nature's playground
boys learn the skills of men

there's comfort in her eyes
the chewing of her cud
her unhurried plod
to field and lane
companions
head for home

to the chirring song of cart-wheels
not knowing the words
but in tune
he sings

as in a dance they circle					forking lifting fluffing

shaking loose each dew-damp stem　　　threshing can begin

yoked for life
mother daughter
a gift of blood

one hundred miles inland   high on that hillside   came the sigh of the sea the hiss of the tide

the song of wood gliding grain   as it has for three thousand years before   the threshing floor comes to life once more

scattered coronets

across the threshing floor   tell of work well done

with hat in hand
the sun on my face
though I have no whip to
urge on my cows
I am a charioteer

round and around   drifting nowhere but   the edges of my mind

free falling   never reaching   circle's end

a humble man
through whose eyes I learn to read
the language ploughed into the land

was it but yesterday
we ploughed

sowed the land field by field
now today garner each golden ear

I'll walk with you
to the ends of the earth my faithful friend

weep when you breathe
your earthly last

always the jokers
who wouldn't laugh
with them

treading straw beside their cows
and each grain falls separate on the ground
they pose a moment on their corona

the creak of cartwheels in his eyes
wheat ears sprouting from his hands
ruler of the land he stands upon
he can only smile

families sharing a ride together

how can harmony not prevail

with every spin
clouds of flying chaff
no stones remain

garnering the waterfall of grain							my family want for nothing

sixteen grain crammed sacks
a year's reward
bread enough to feed a family

... and hay flies into the loft
fodder for winter

aye aye aye aye
late into the night
we drink   we sing
each glass
each song
a buttress
against the morrow

within my
open arms
I have
nothing but
my heart
to offer
what more can
a man give

seeing everything around him
I close my eyes
see what the blind man sees
yoked cows
the wooden cart they pull
the brandy bottle on the table

*though just four foot I may be
and my overcoat too big
I am el rey
I am the king*

what's mine is yours
so what can I get you my friend

loosened from earth
moon's orb
peeks low
rests a moment

on the horizon
watching the antics below
gear into
full swing

unaware for what they wait
on a lone rock I came upon them
a flock of cormorants gazing at the pathless sky

scattered beneath
the poplars
treading
light pools   gold
rains about them

no hurry to be anywhere but exactly here
we chat awhile

a full day's scything over
what a beautiful evening
he calls out cheerily

what light is there no shadow dims
what sky no cloud obscures
suspended within blue-black
day lingers a little while

Acknowledgements

Just Donna and Donna alone, it is thanks to her these photographs have become a book.

If not for her, like windblown leaves their pages would still lie scattered on the floor.

So, thank you Donna for your enthusiastic encouragement, your hard work juggling formats, files and layouts and to me, other incomprehensible stuff.

Also by E.P. Rose:

Poet Under a Soldier's Hat

Ditty Dotty Ditties

portraits: poems

The Perfect Servant... nope

When Cows Wore Shoes

The Long the Short and the Tall

www.galisteoliz.com

www.ingramcontent.com/pod-product-compliance
Lightning Source LLC
Chambersburg PA
CBRC101135130526
44582CB00035B/197